Coloring Lovers Series

GEOMETRIC PATTERNS COLORING BOOK

VOLUME 1

Kristin Preachers

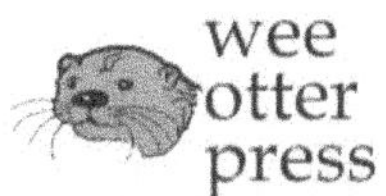

First Printing, 2015

ISBN 978-0-9966921-0-6

Wee Otter Press
Chattanooga, TN
www.weeotterpress.com

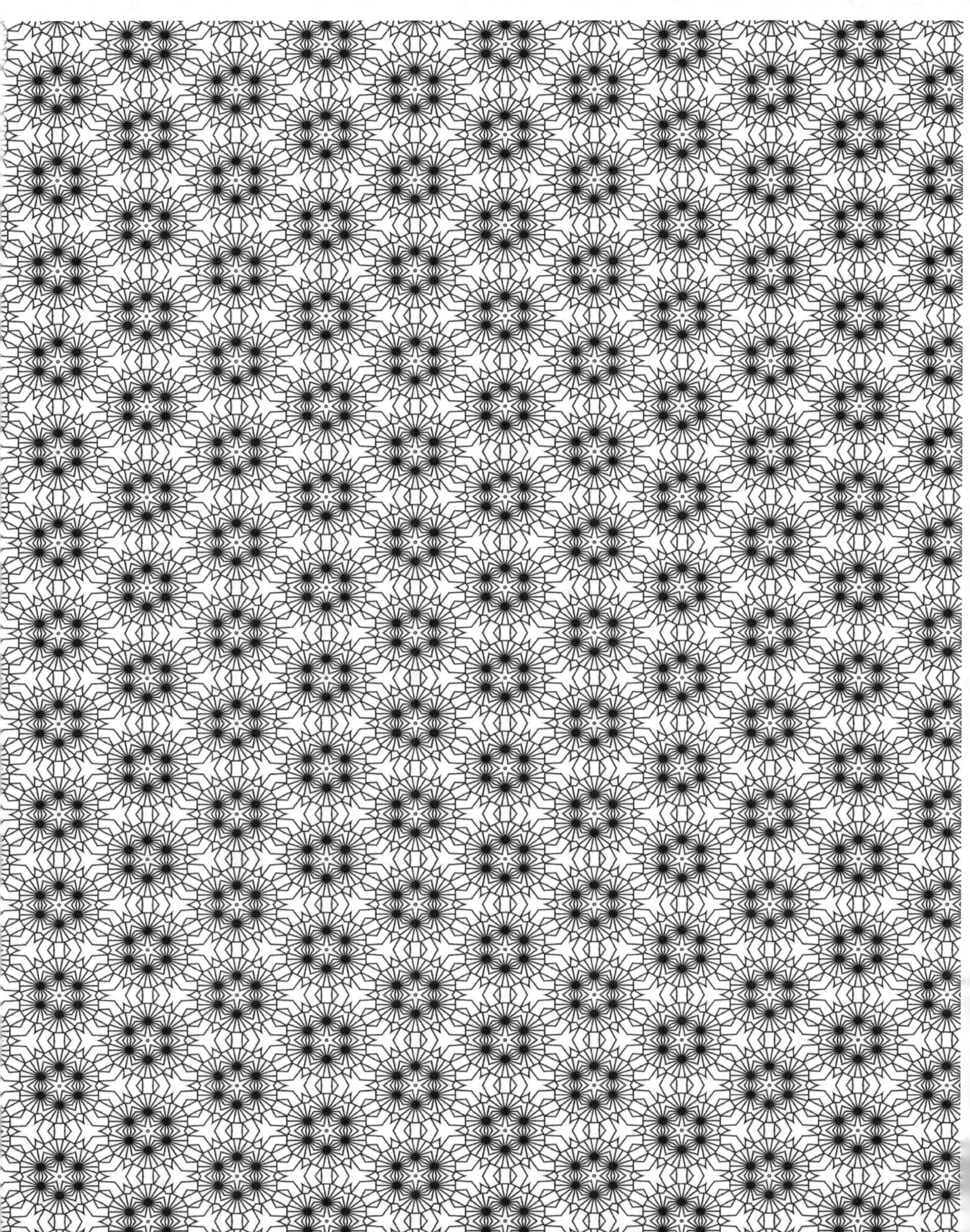

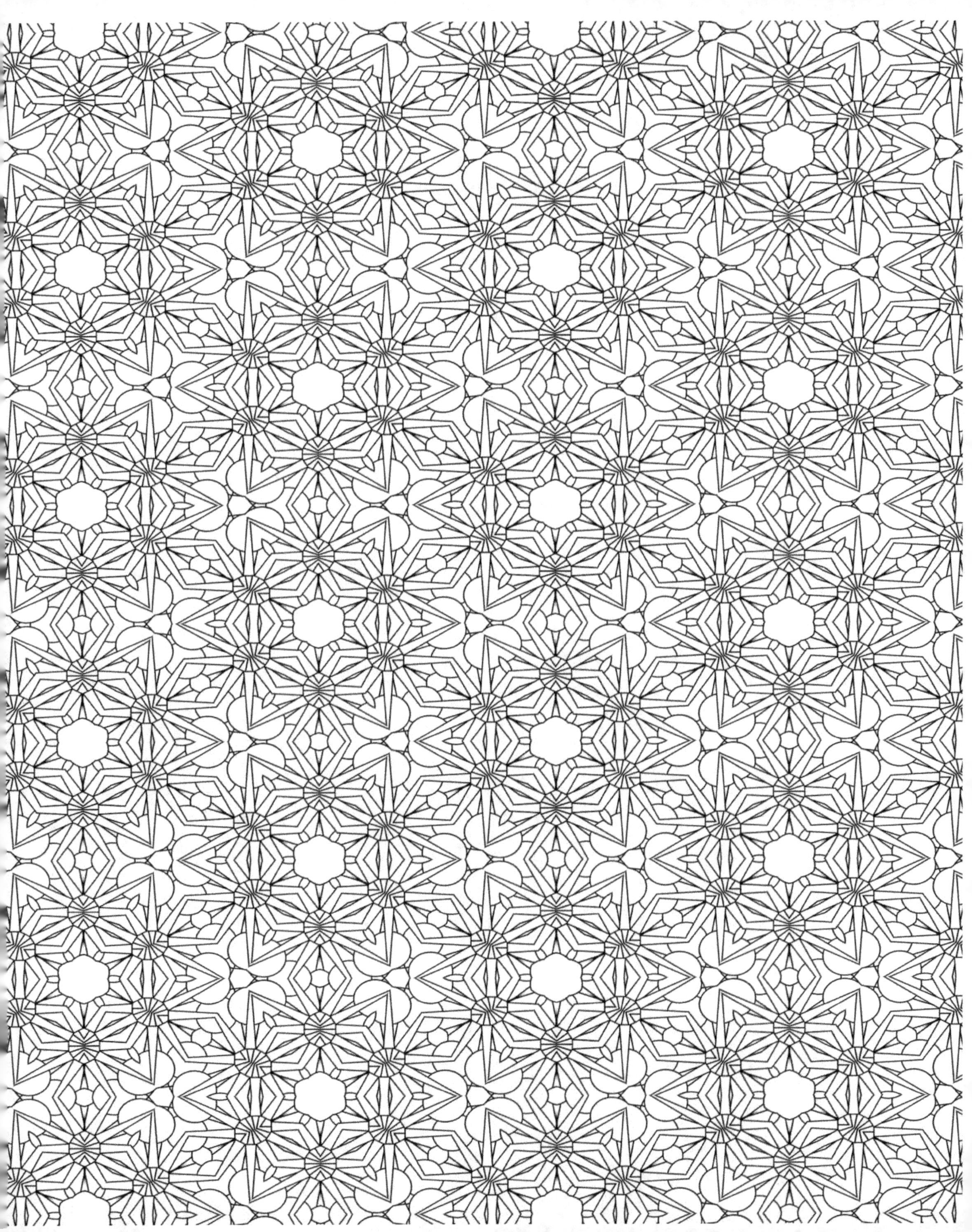

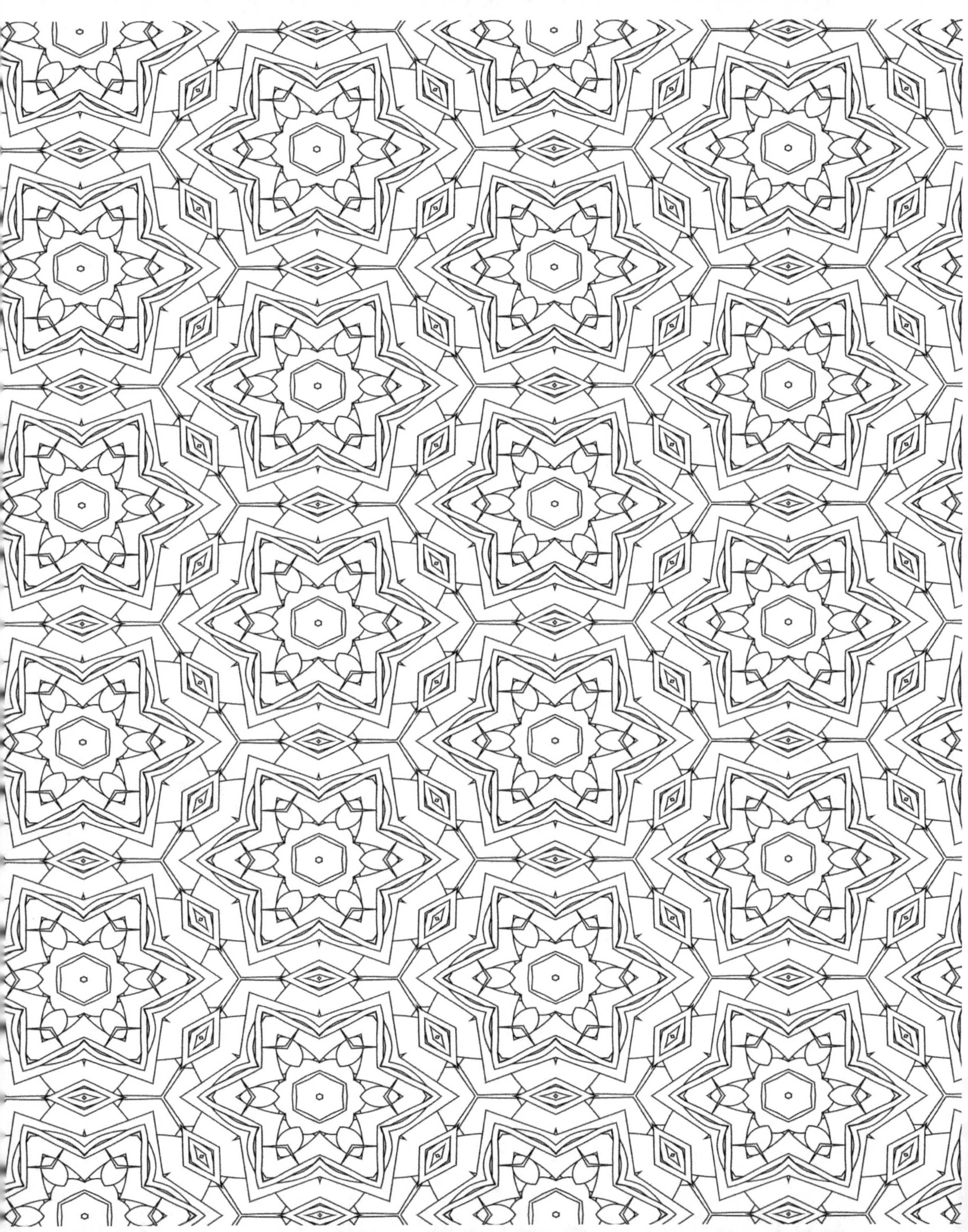

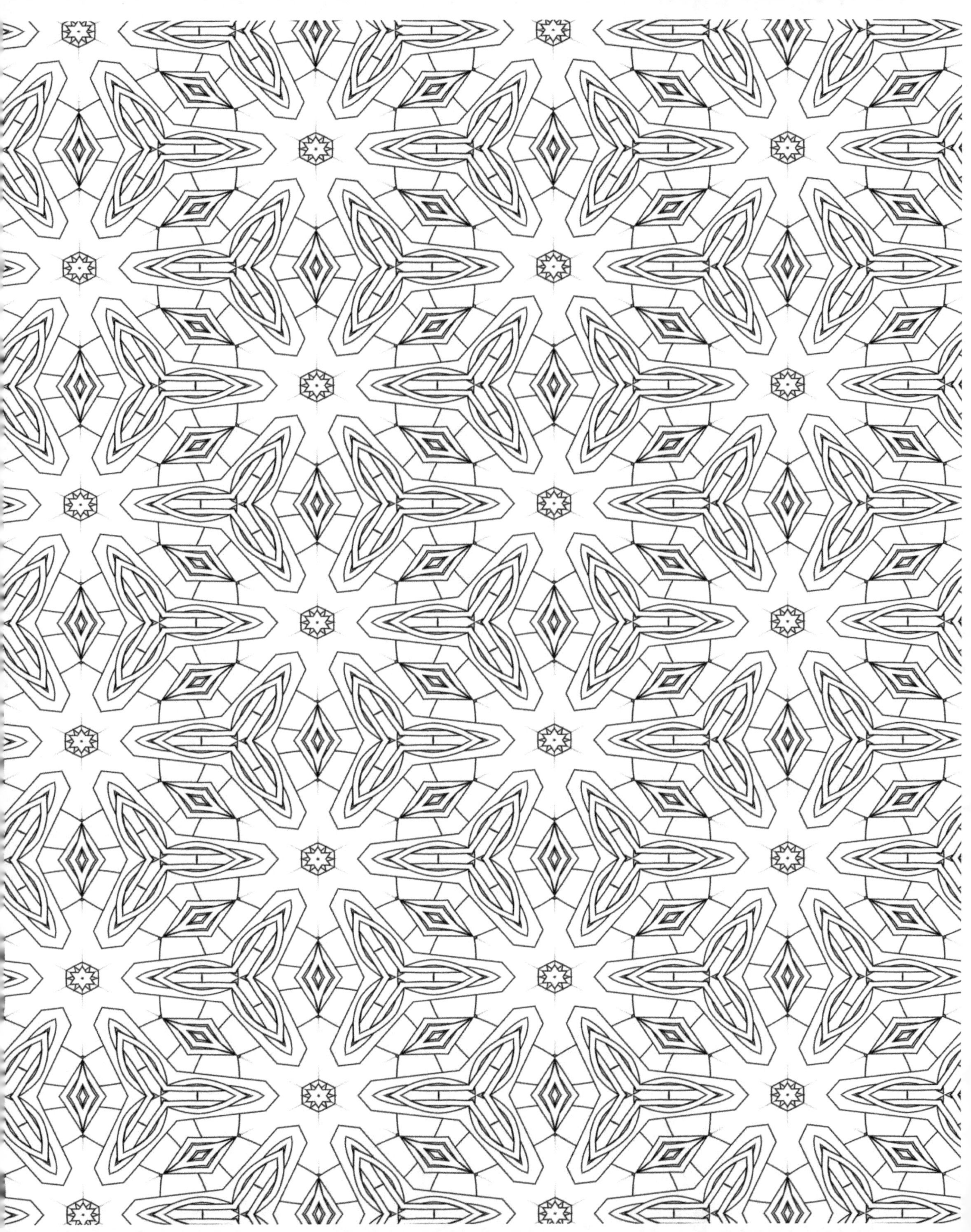

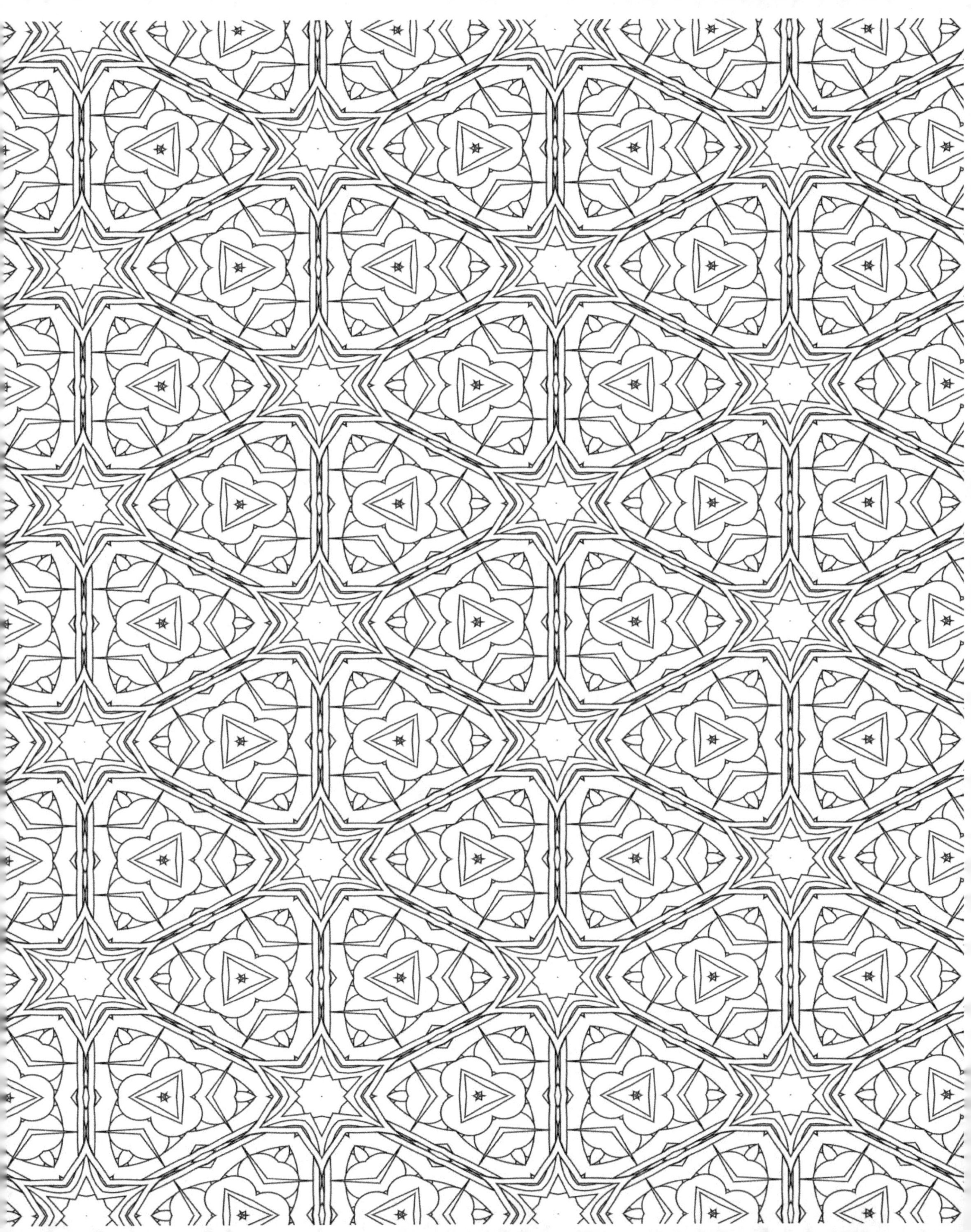

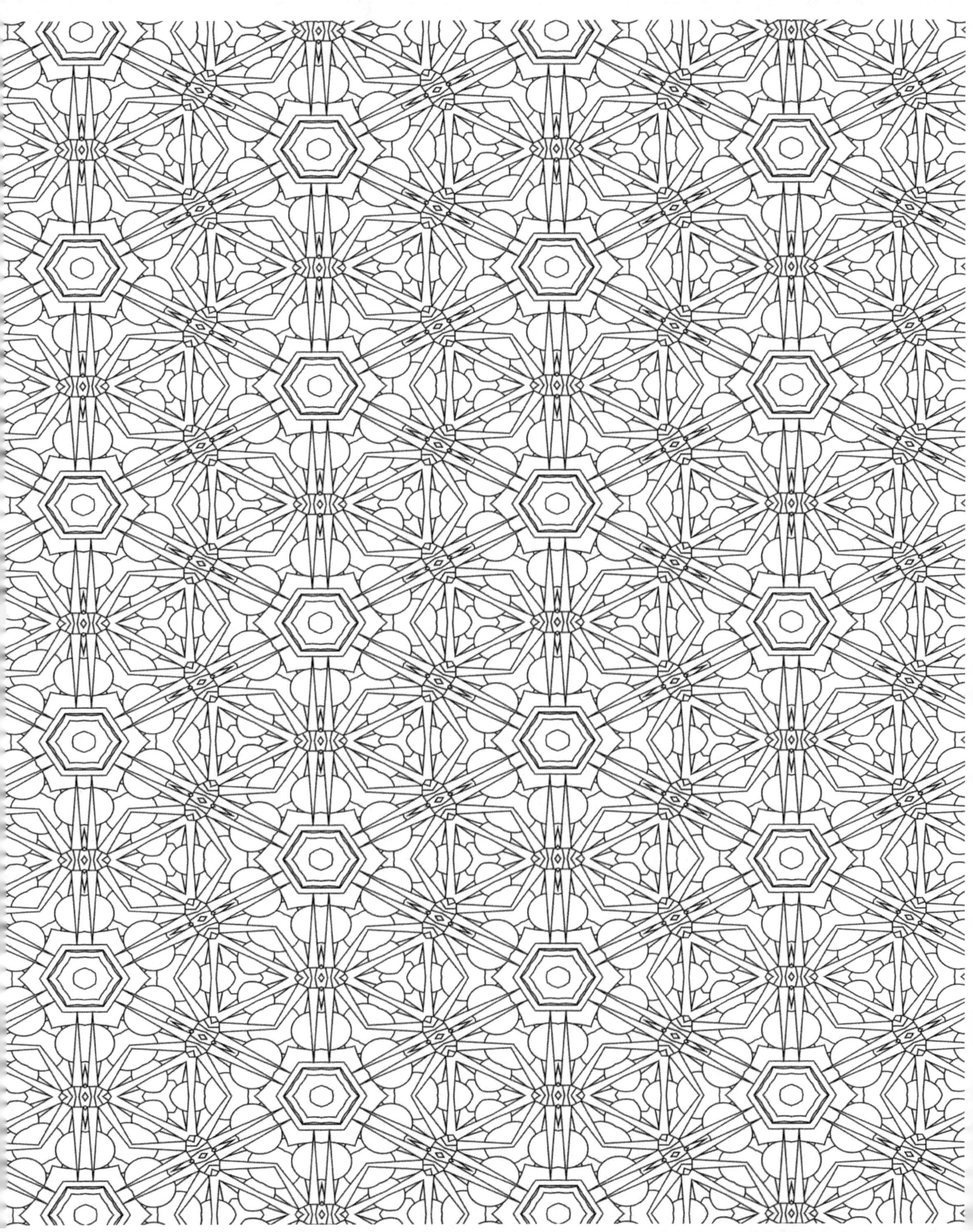

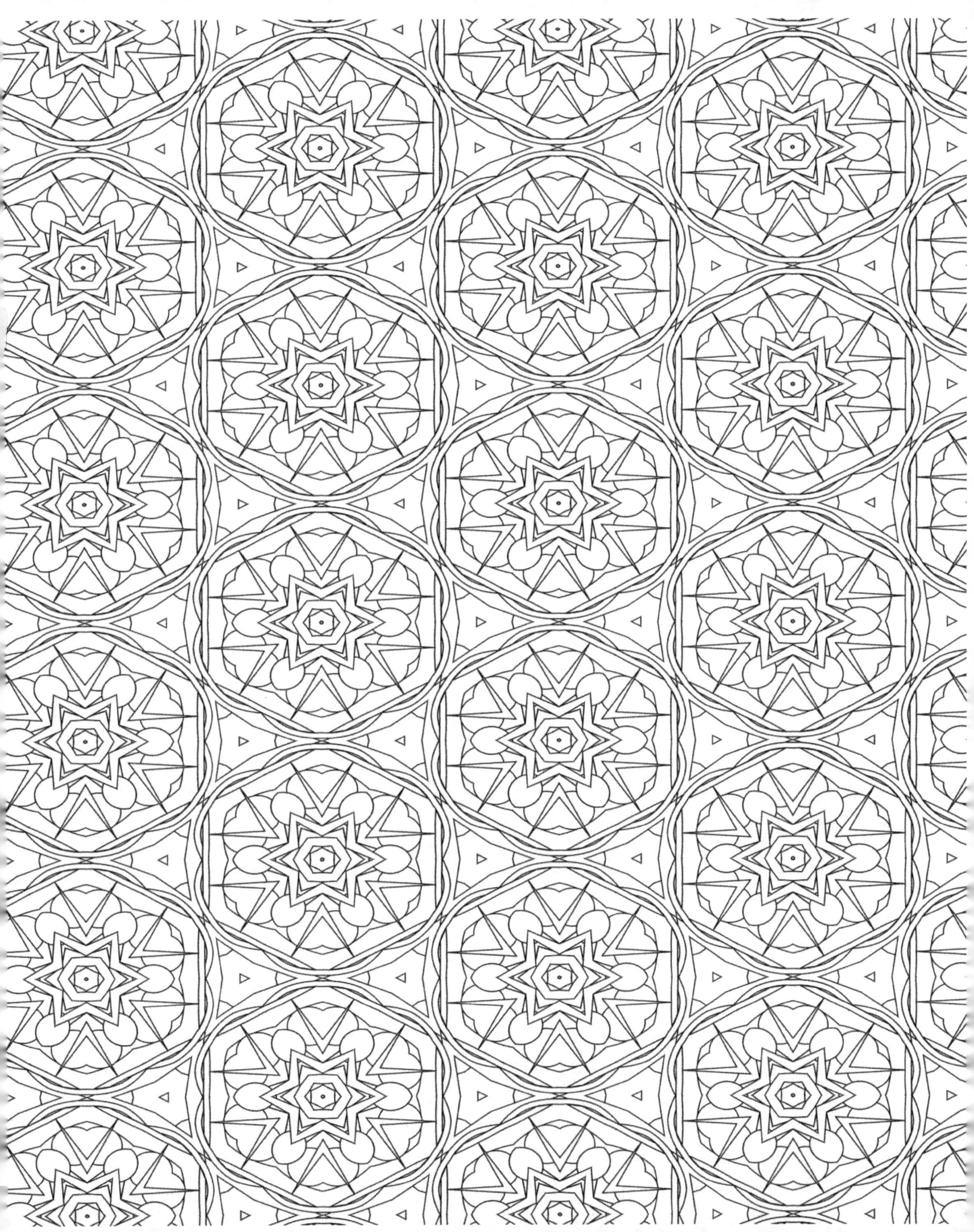

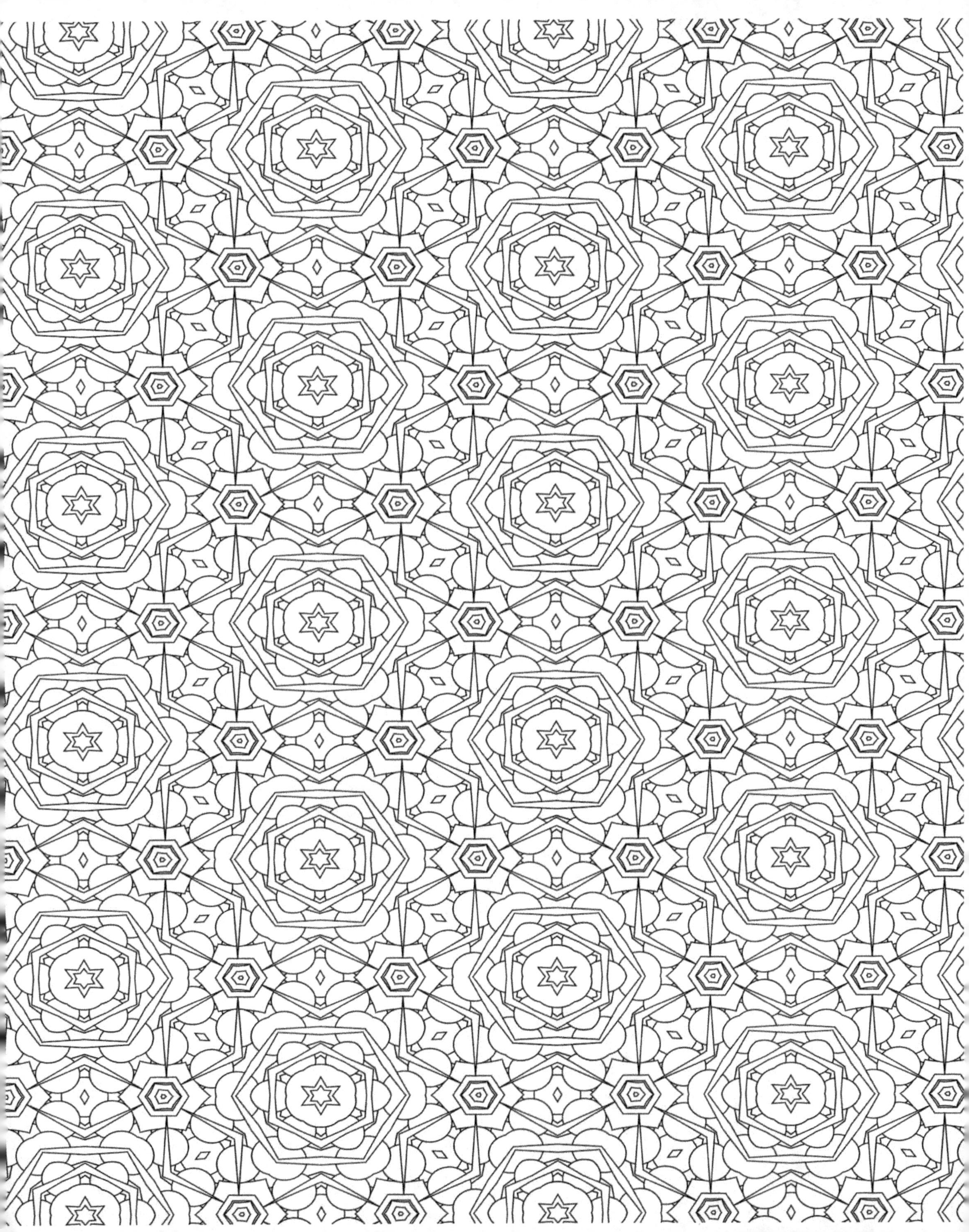

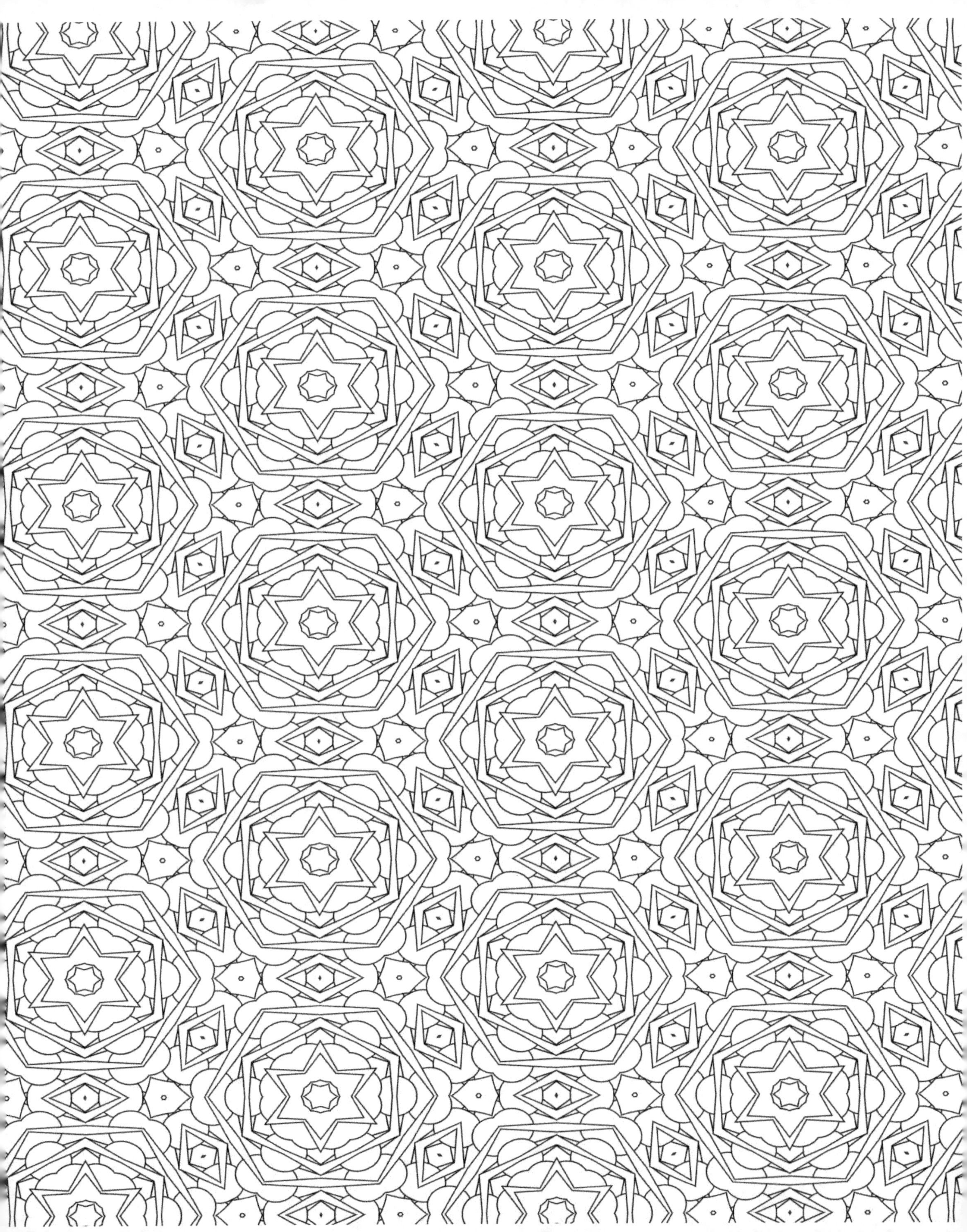

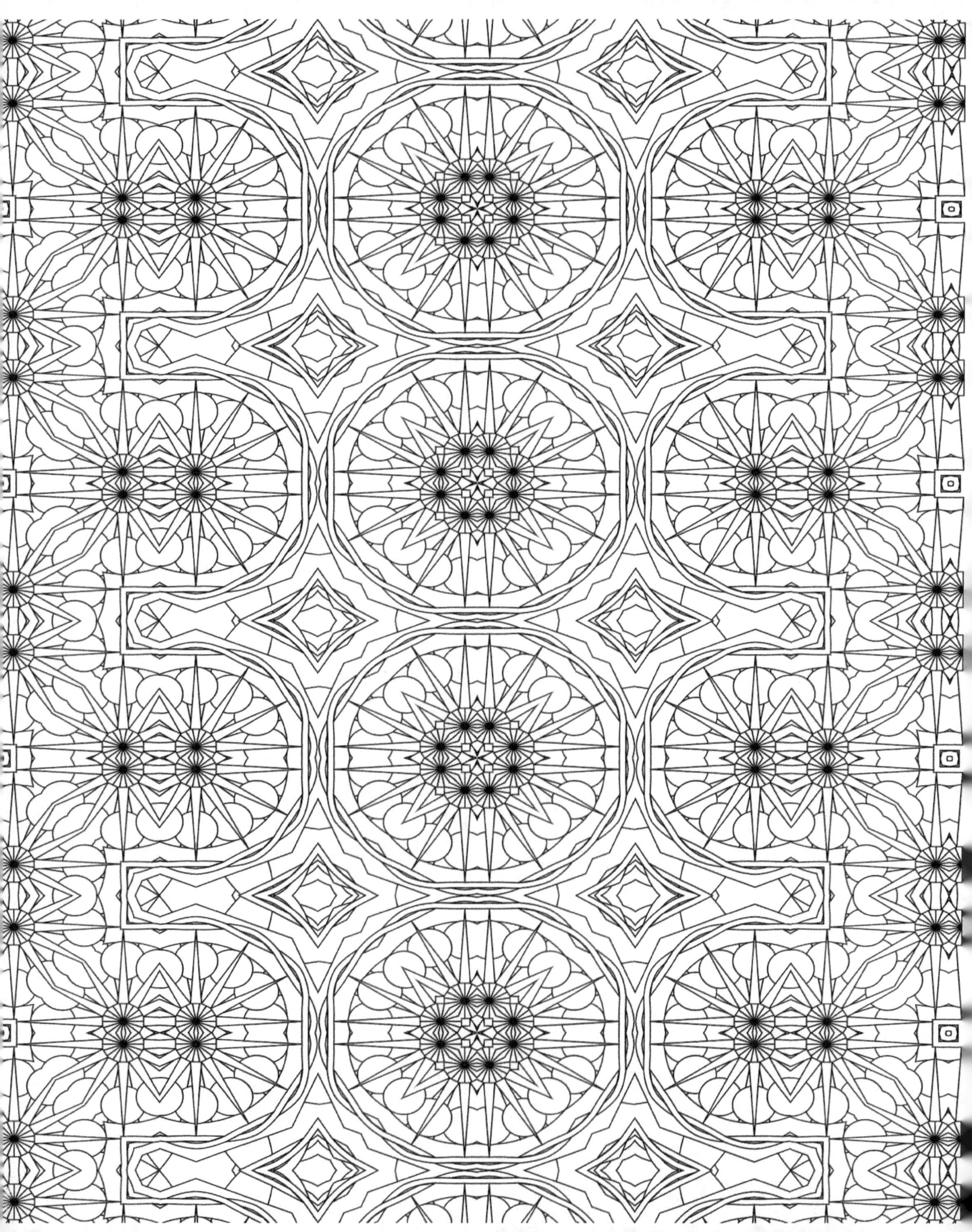

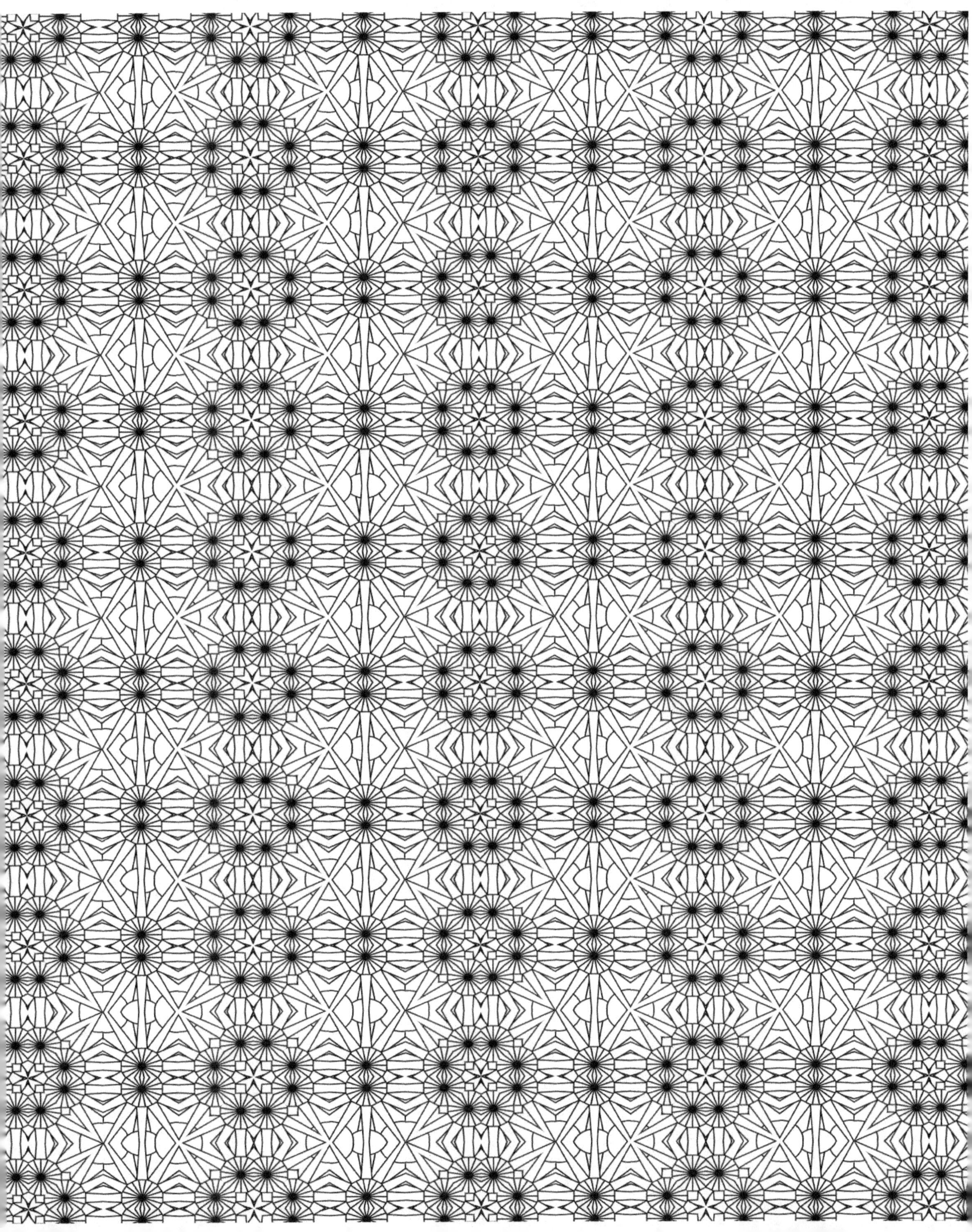

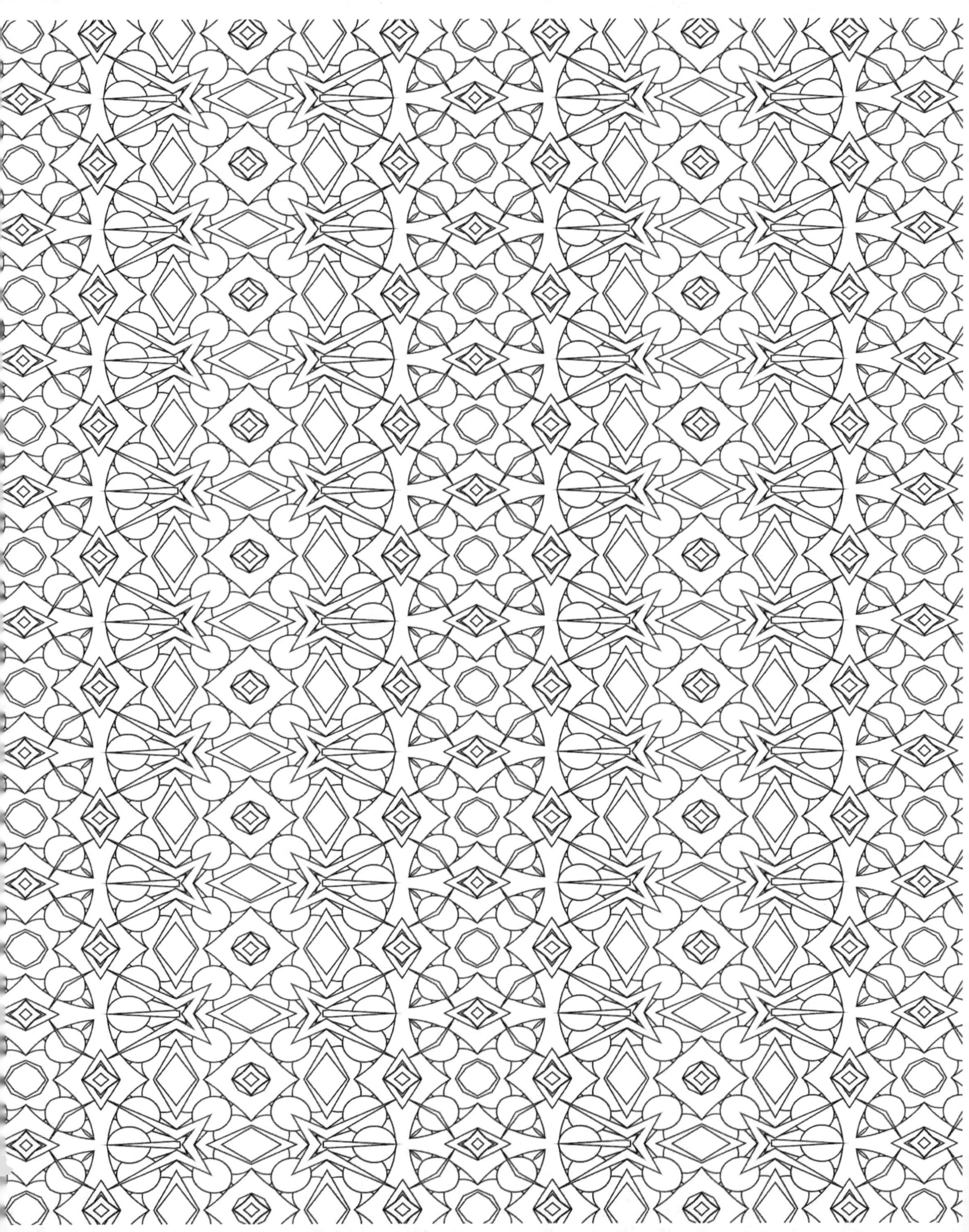

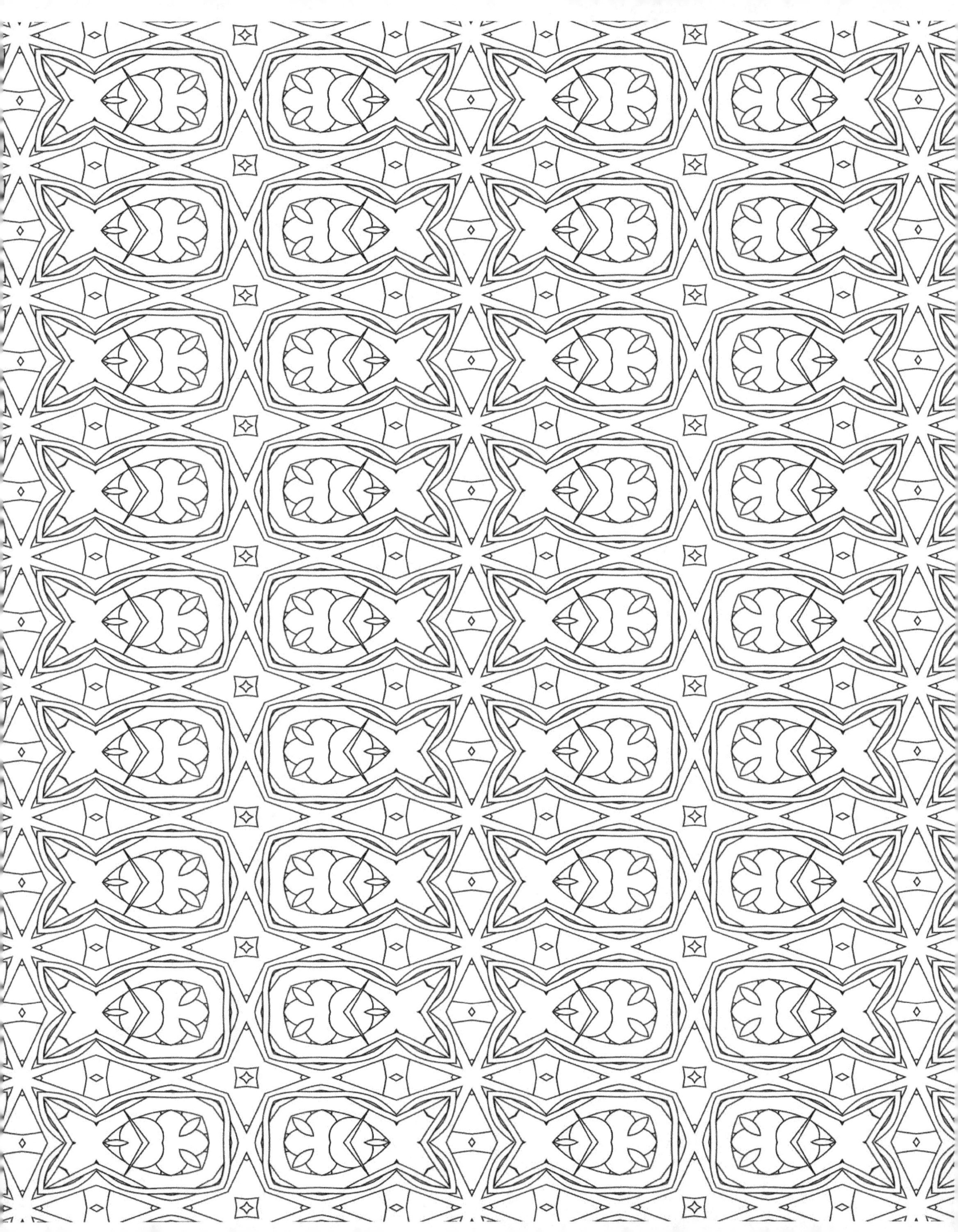

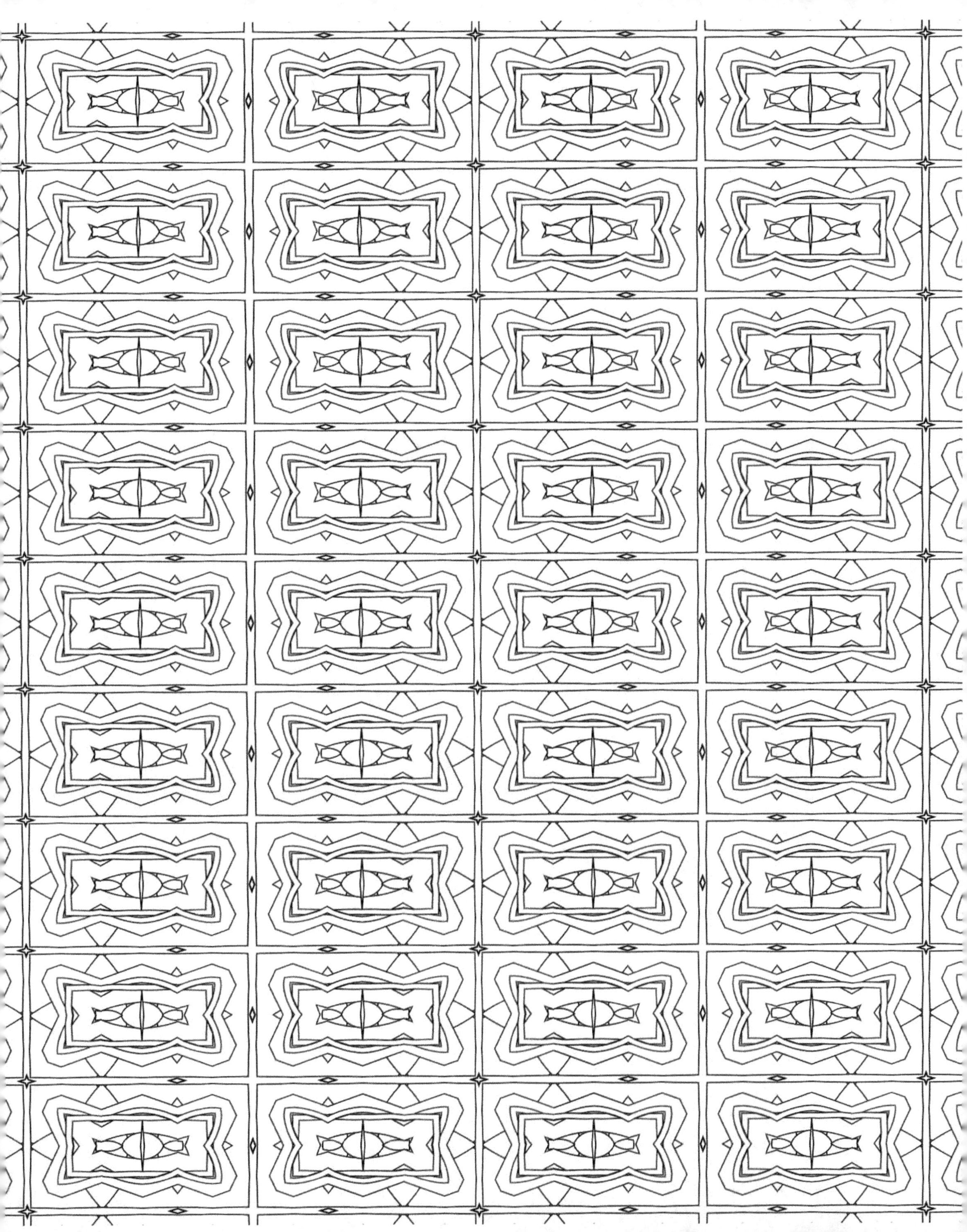

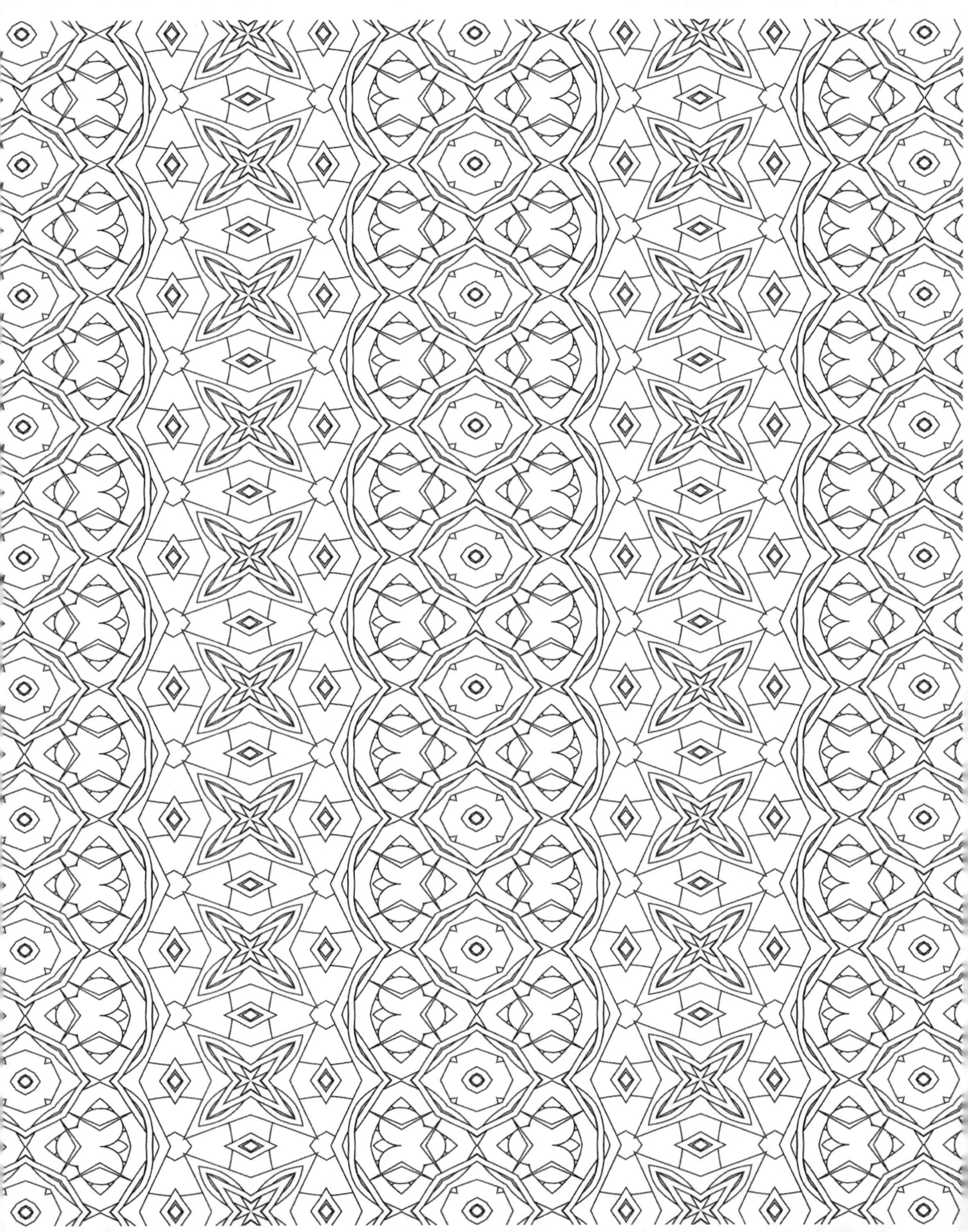

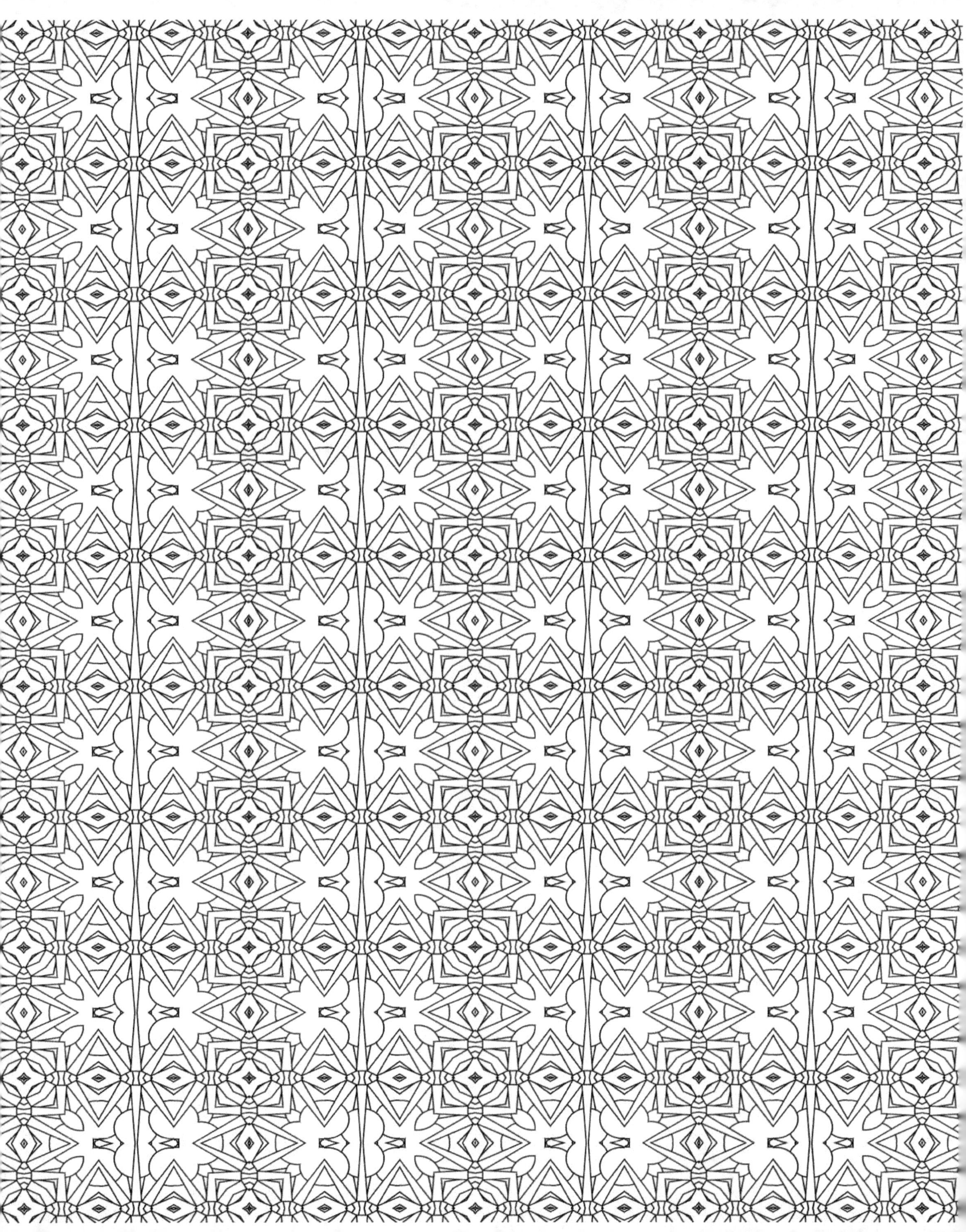

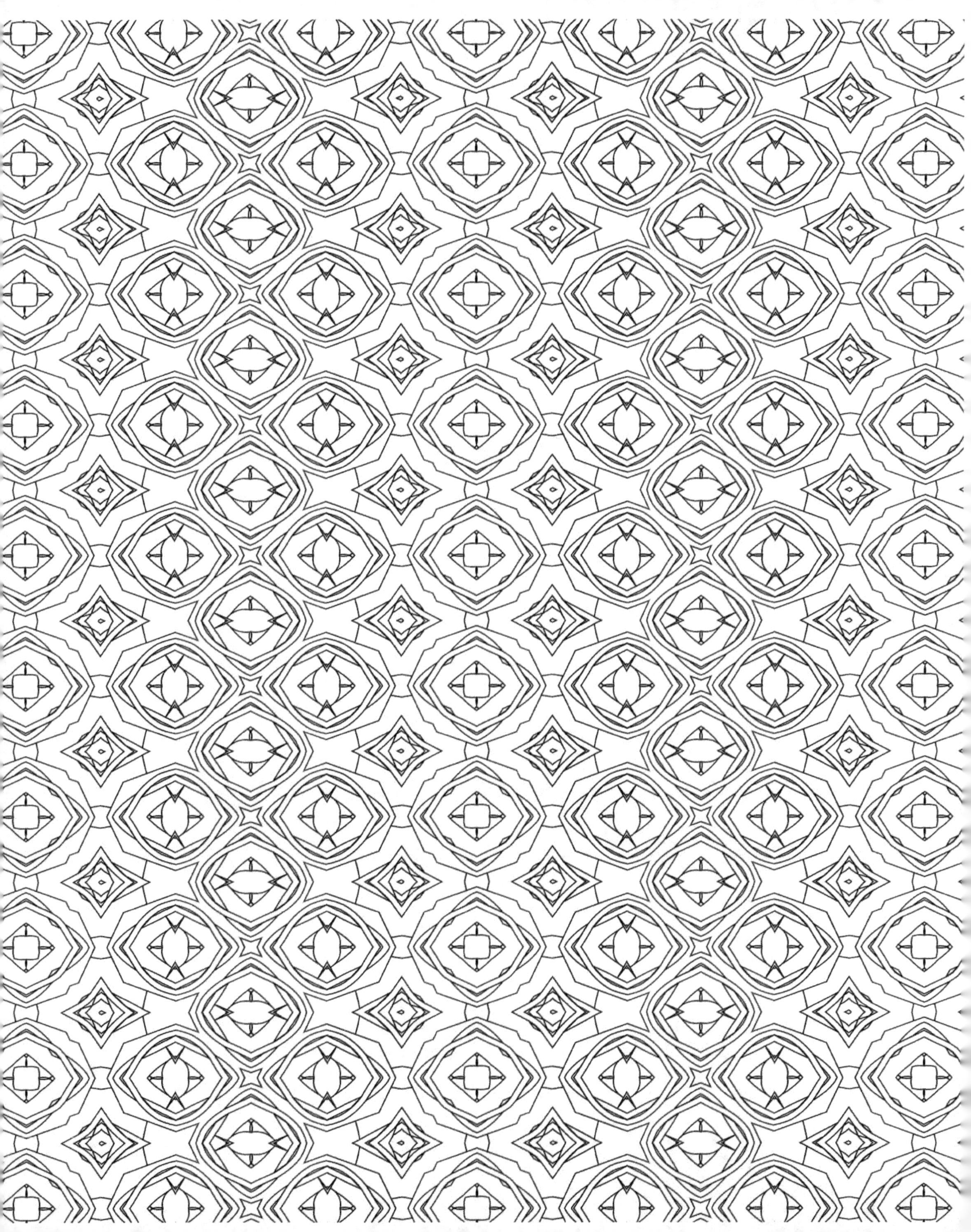

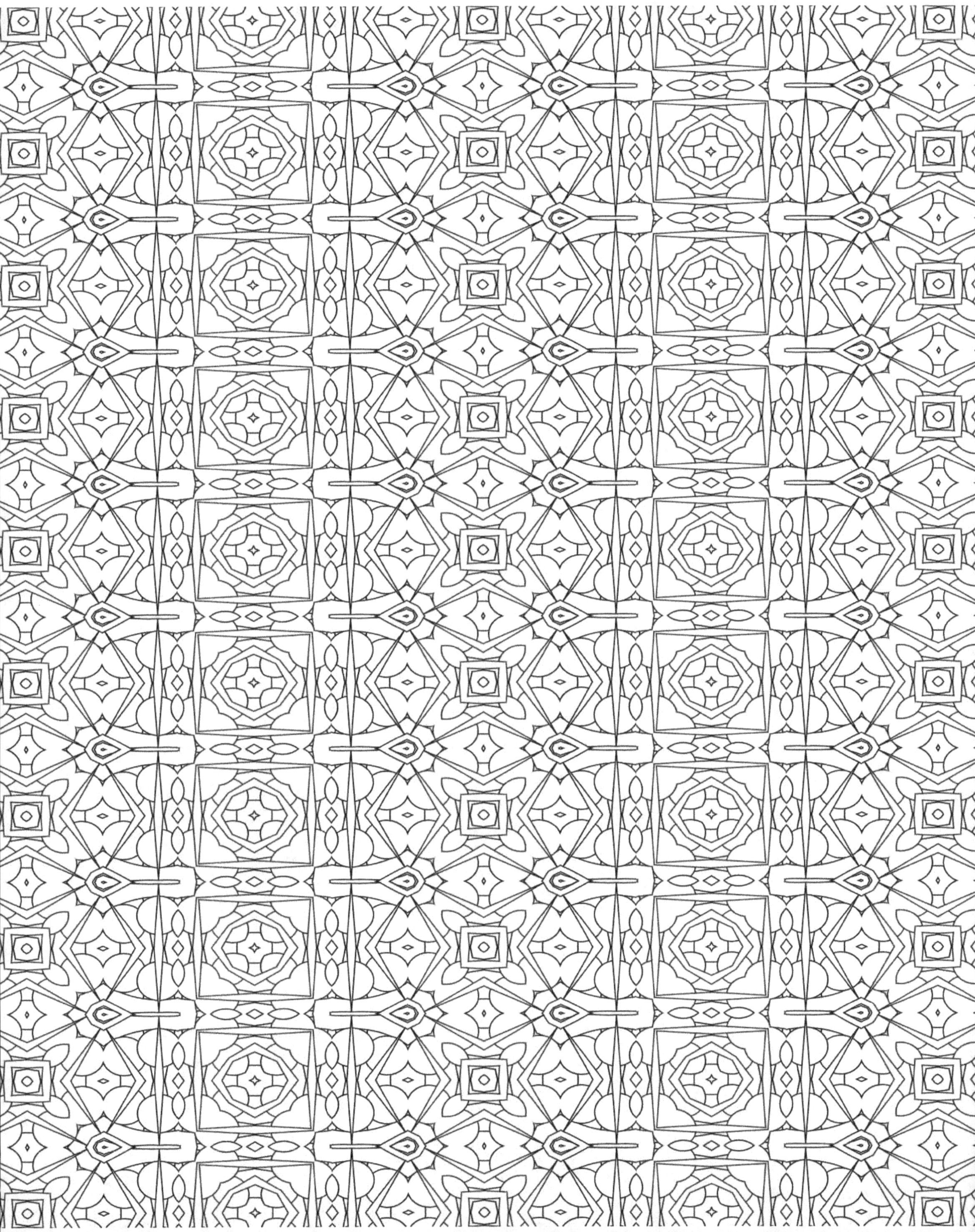

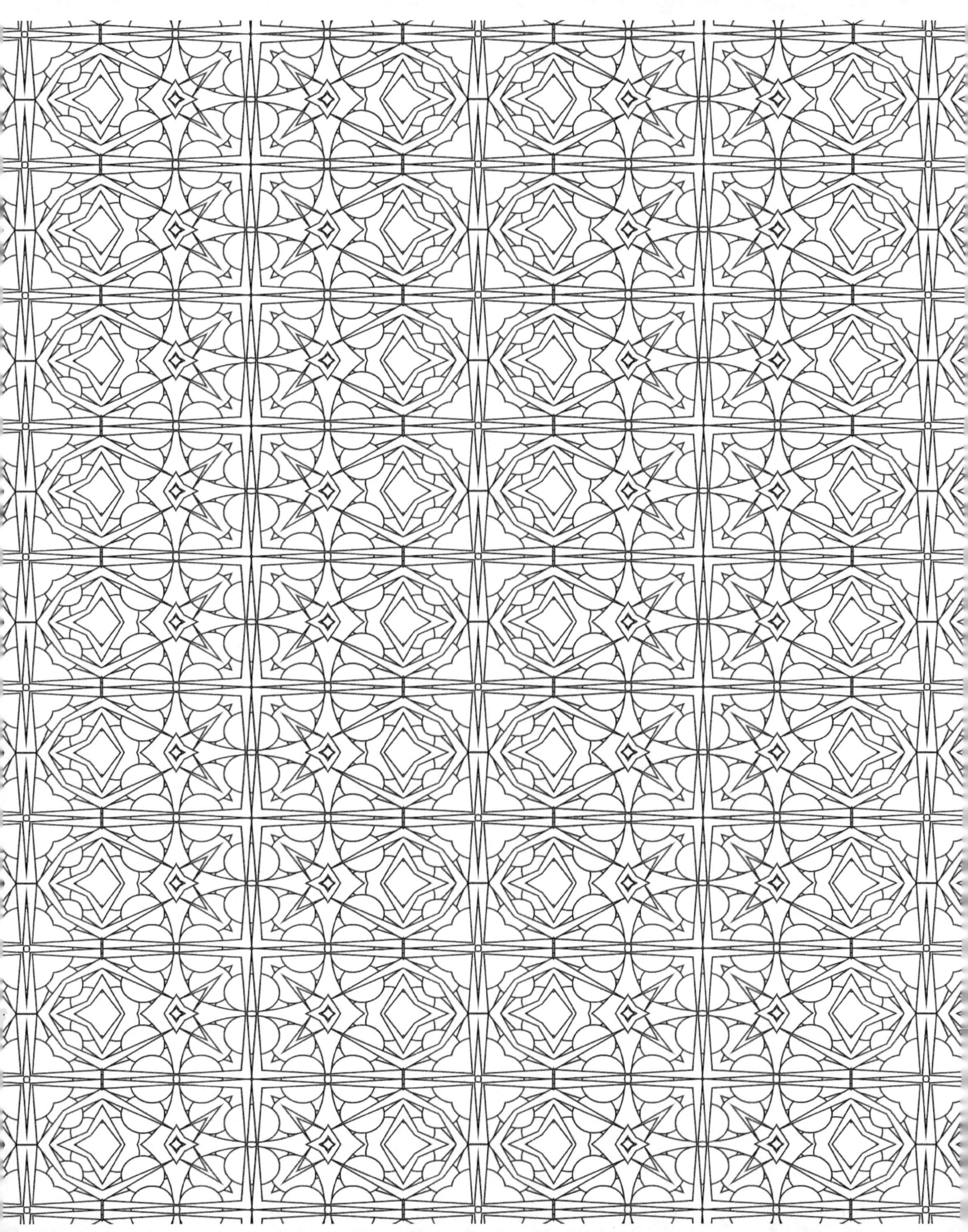

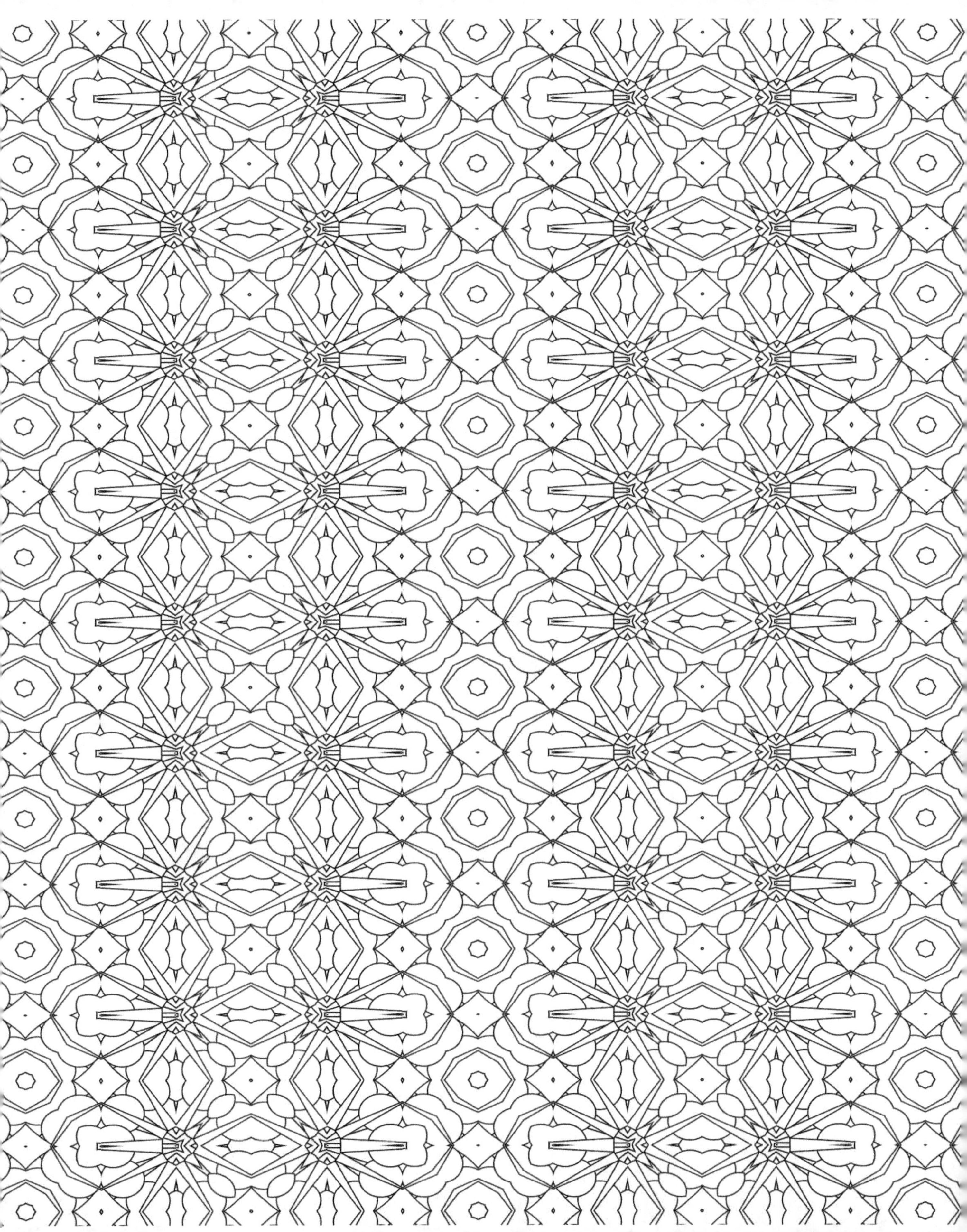

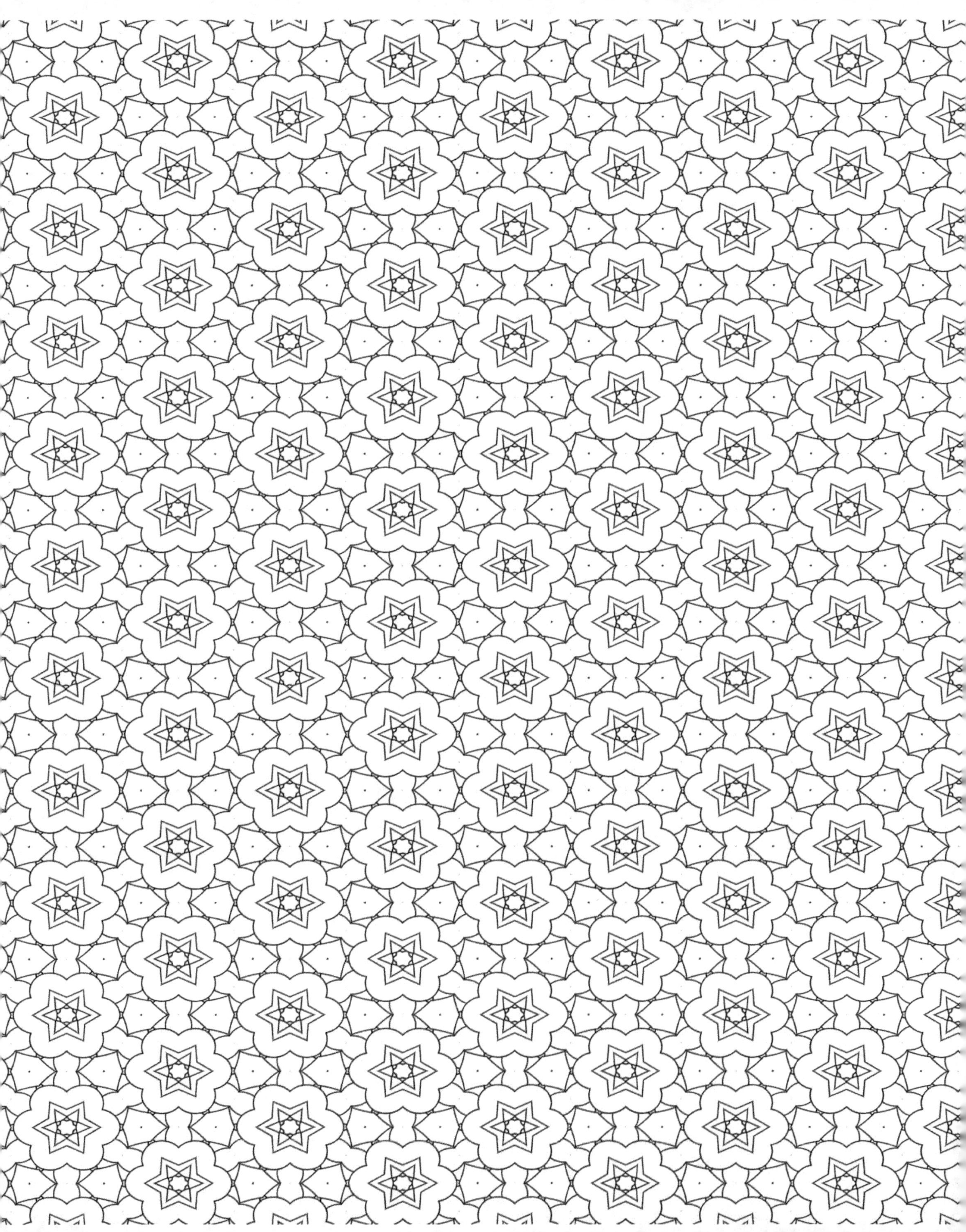

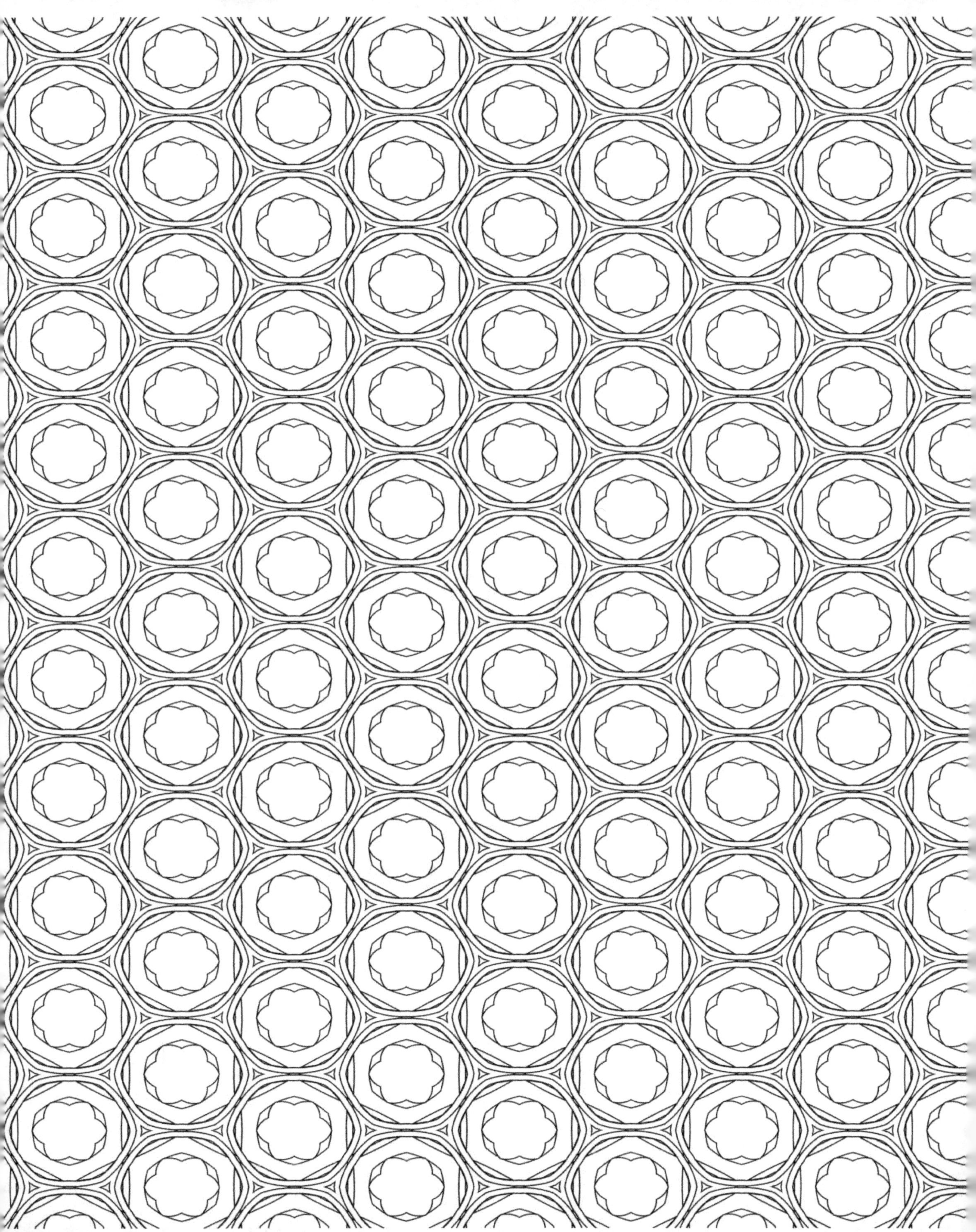

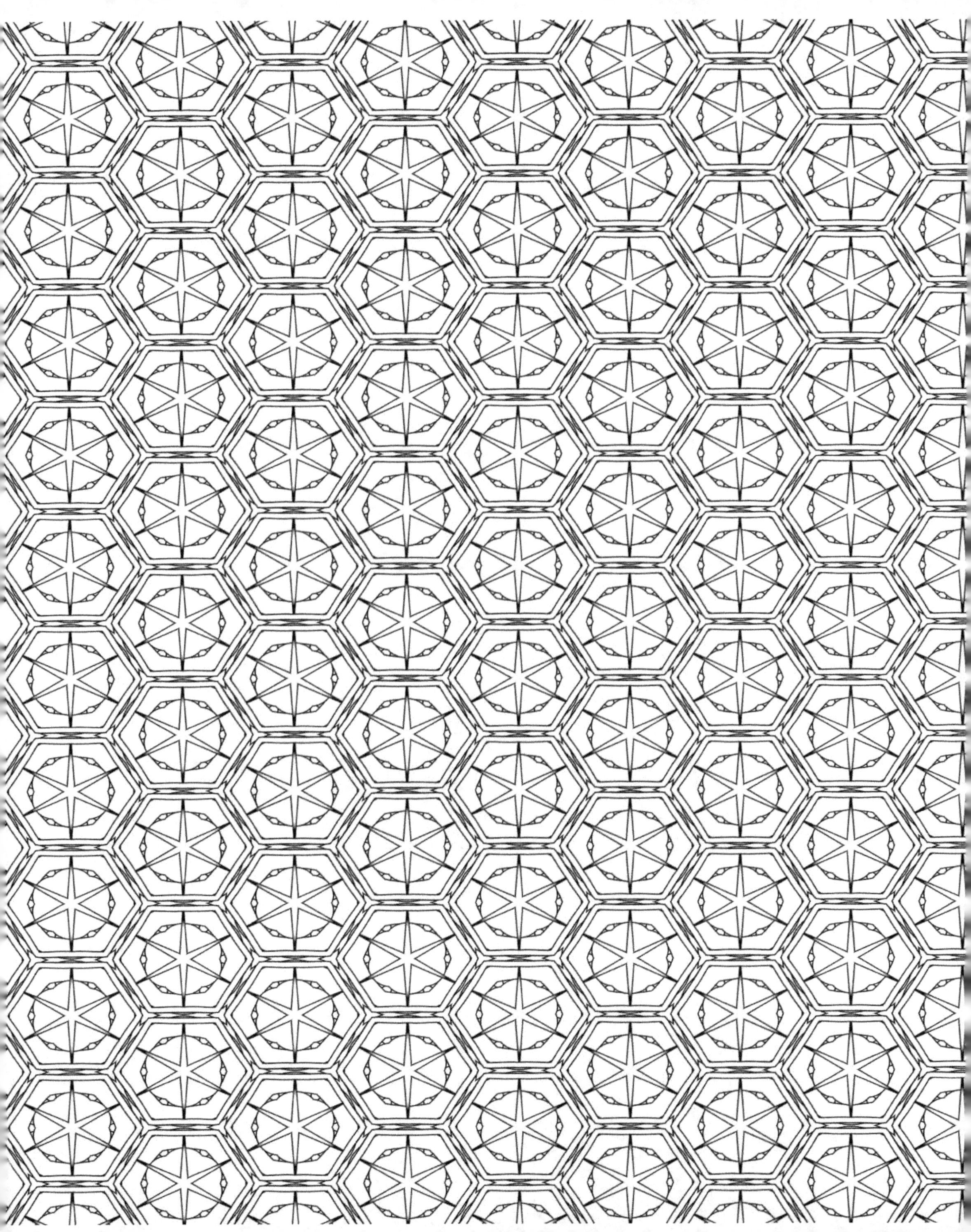

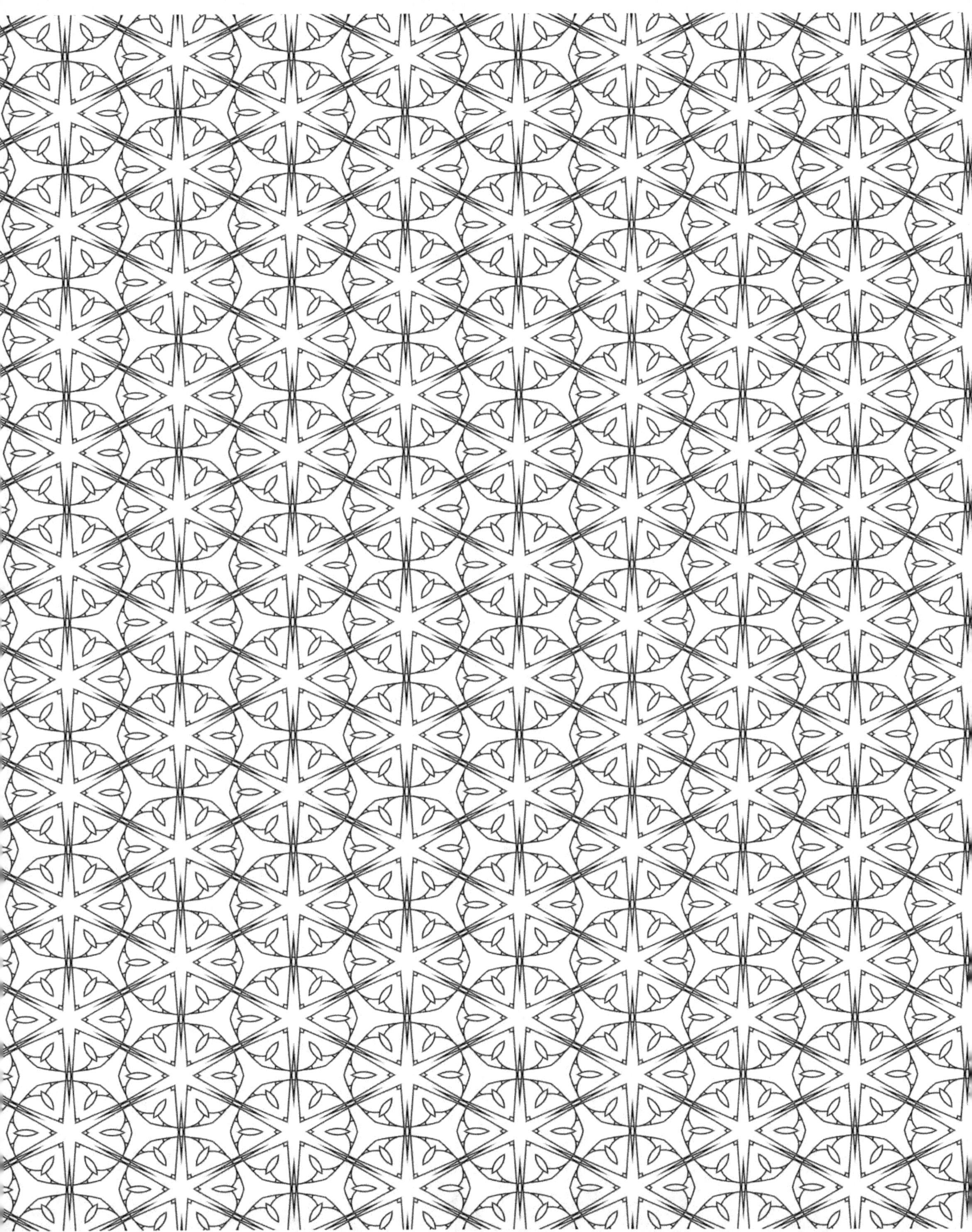

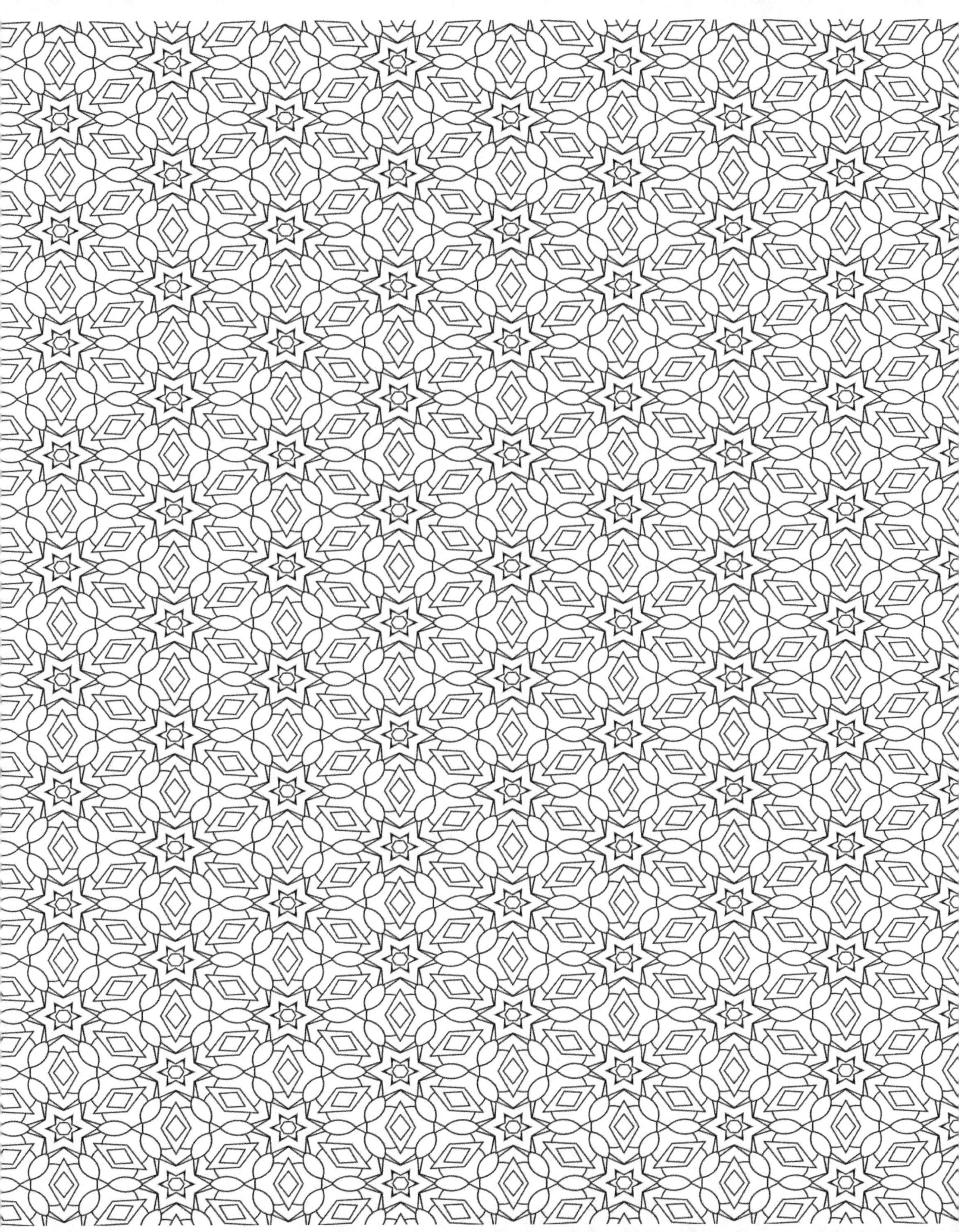

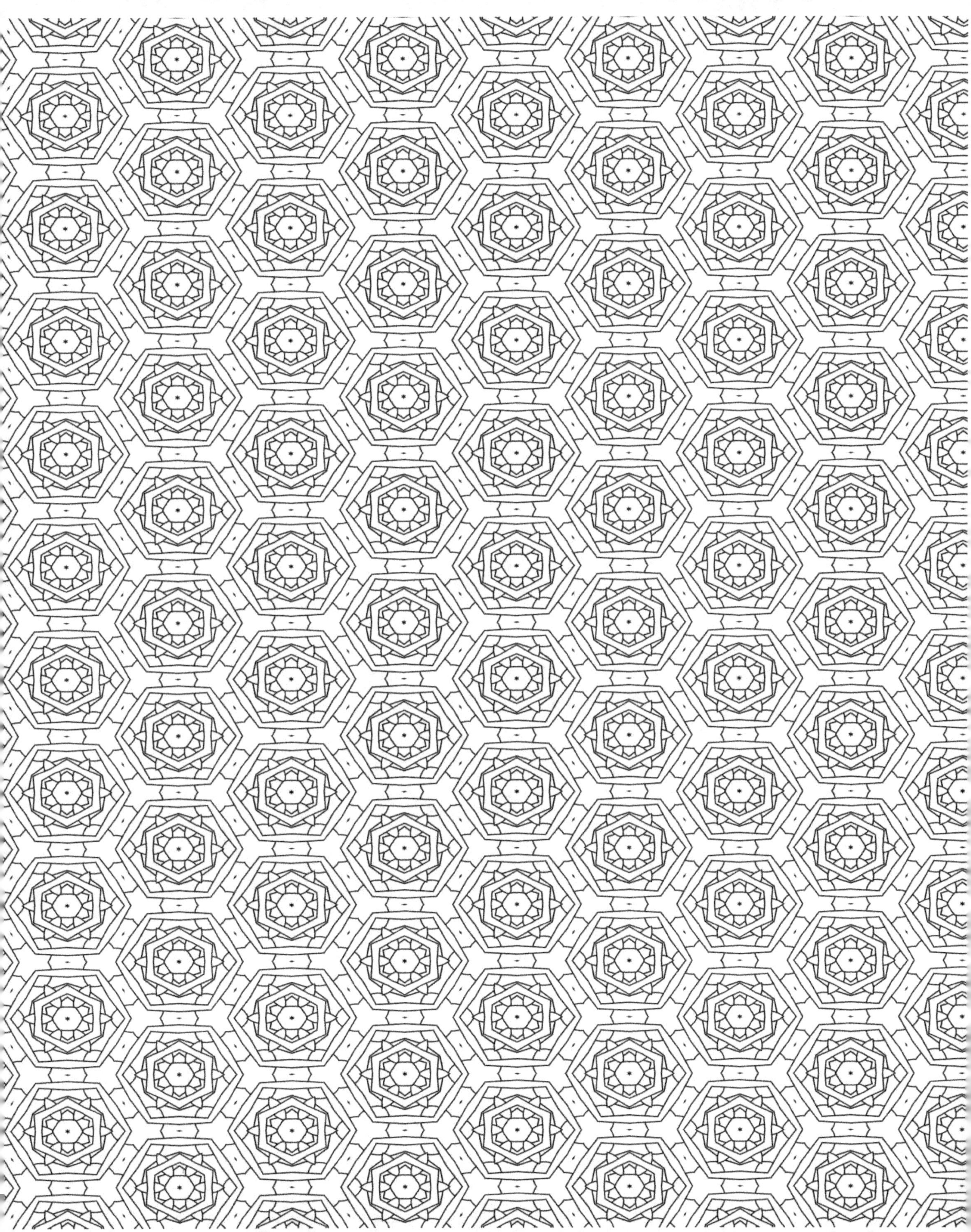

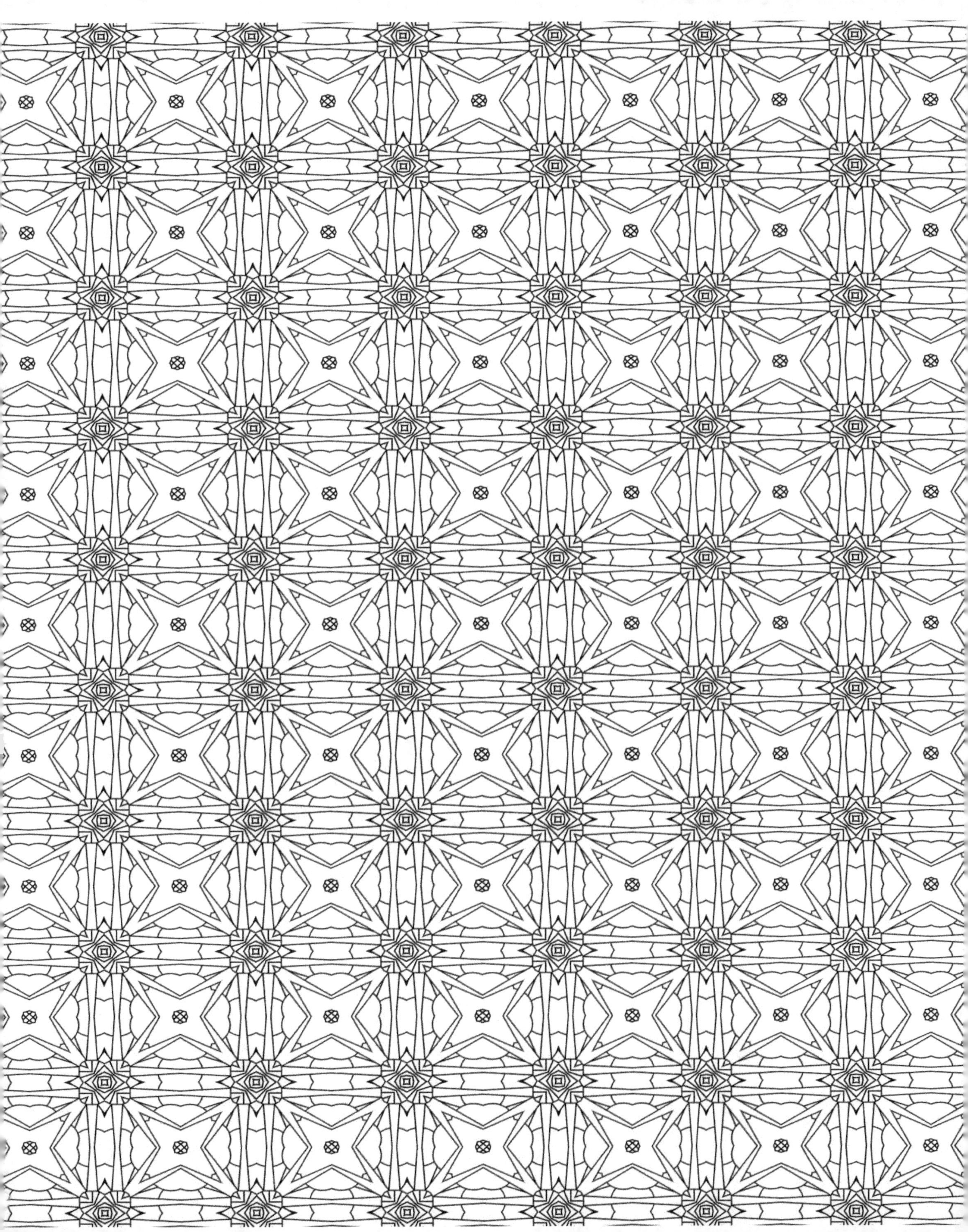

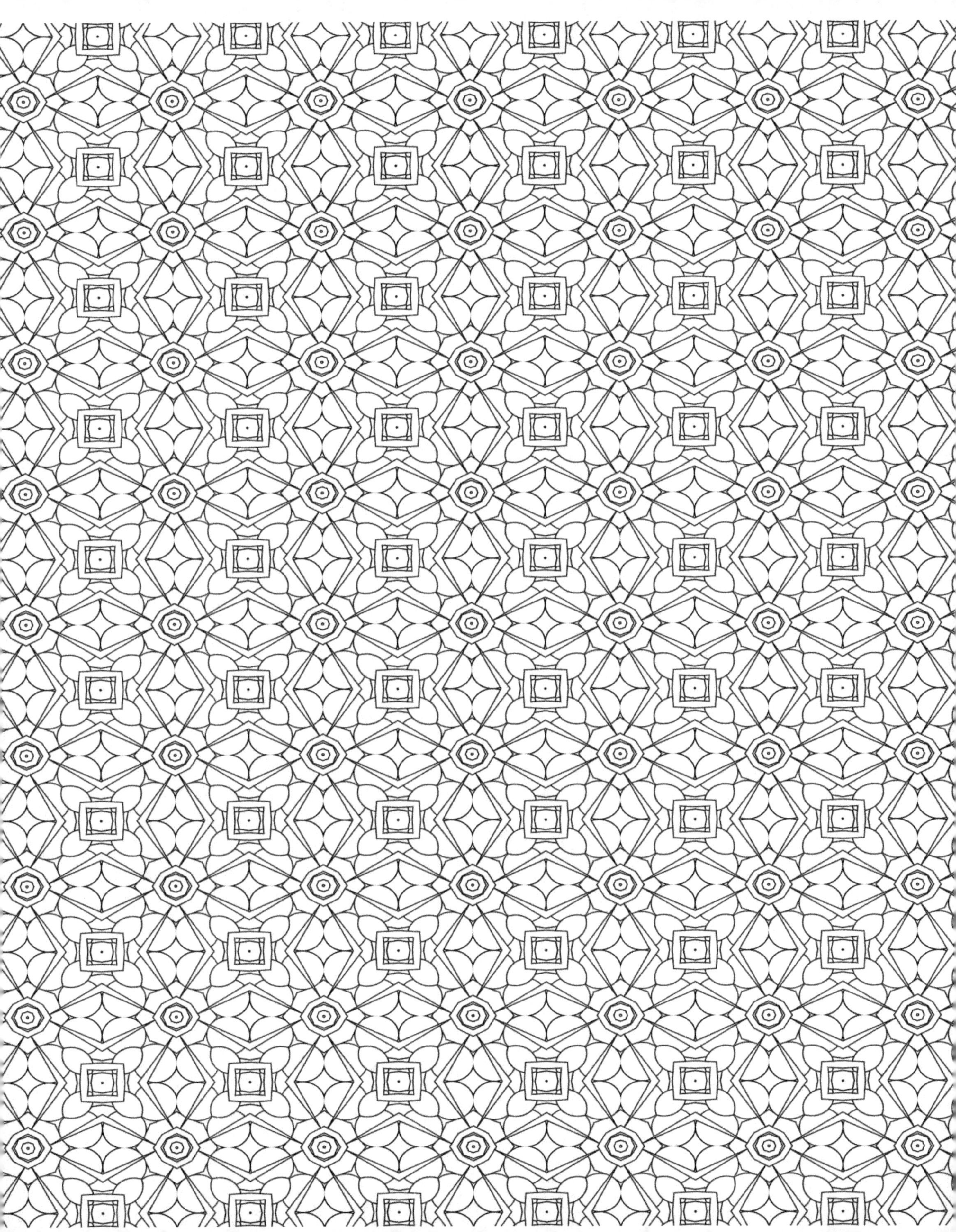

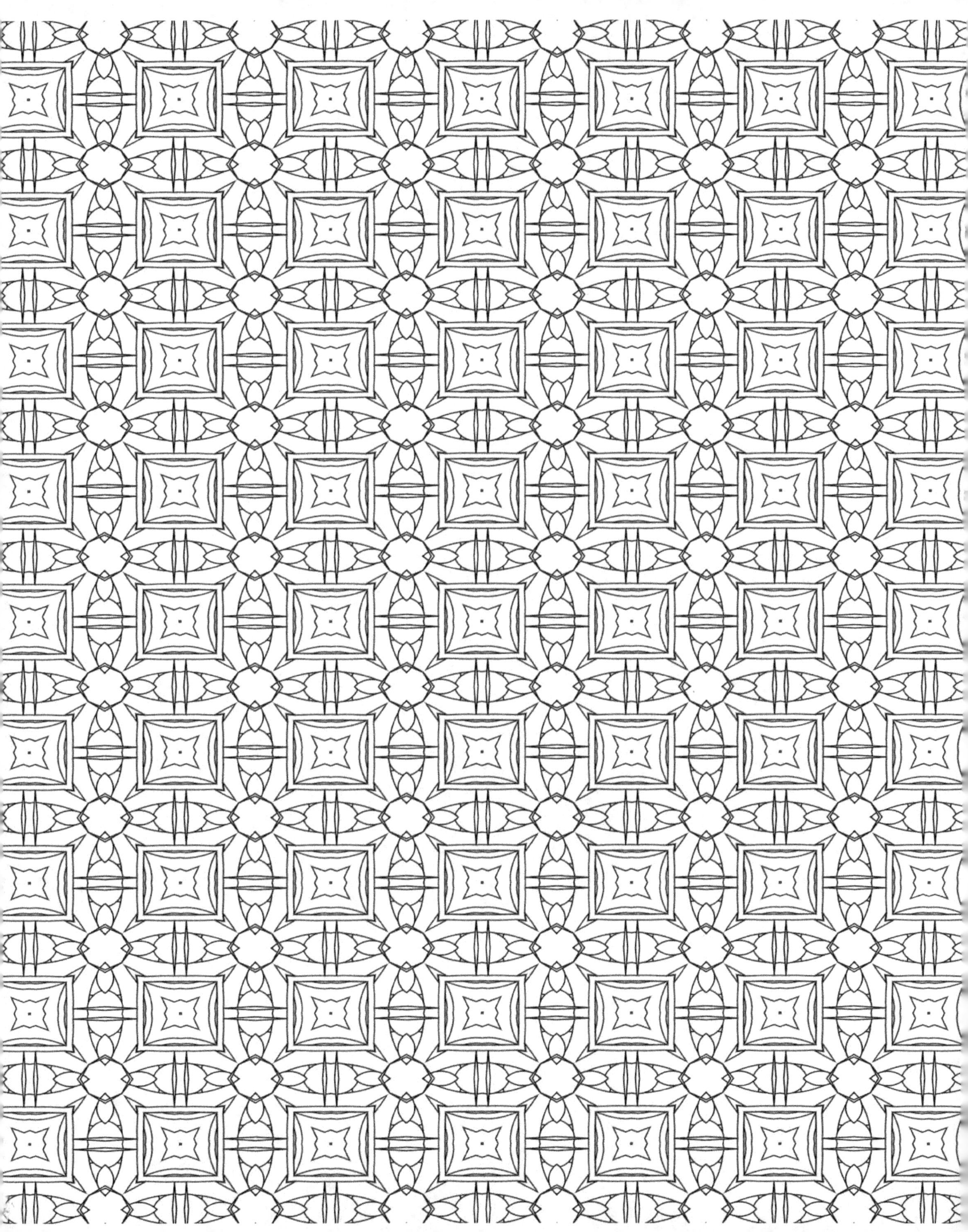

Find more books in the

Coloring Lovers Series:

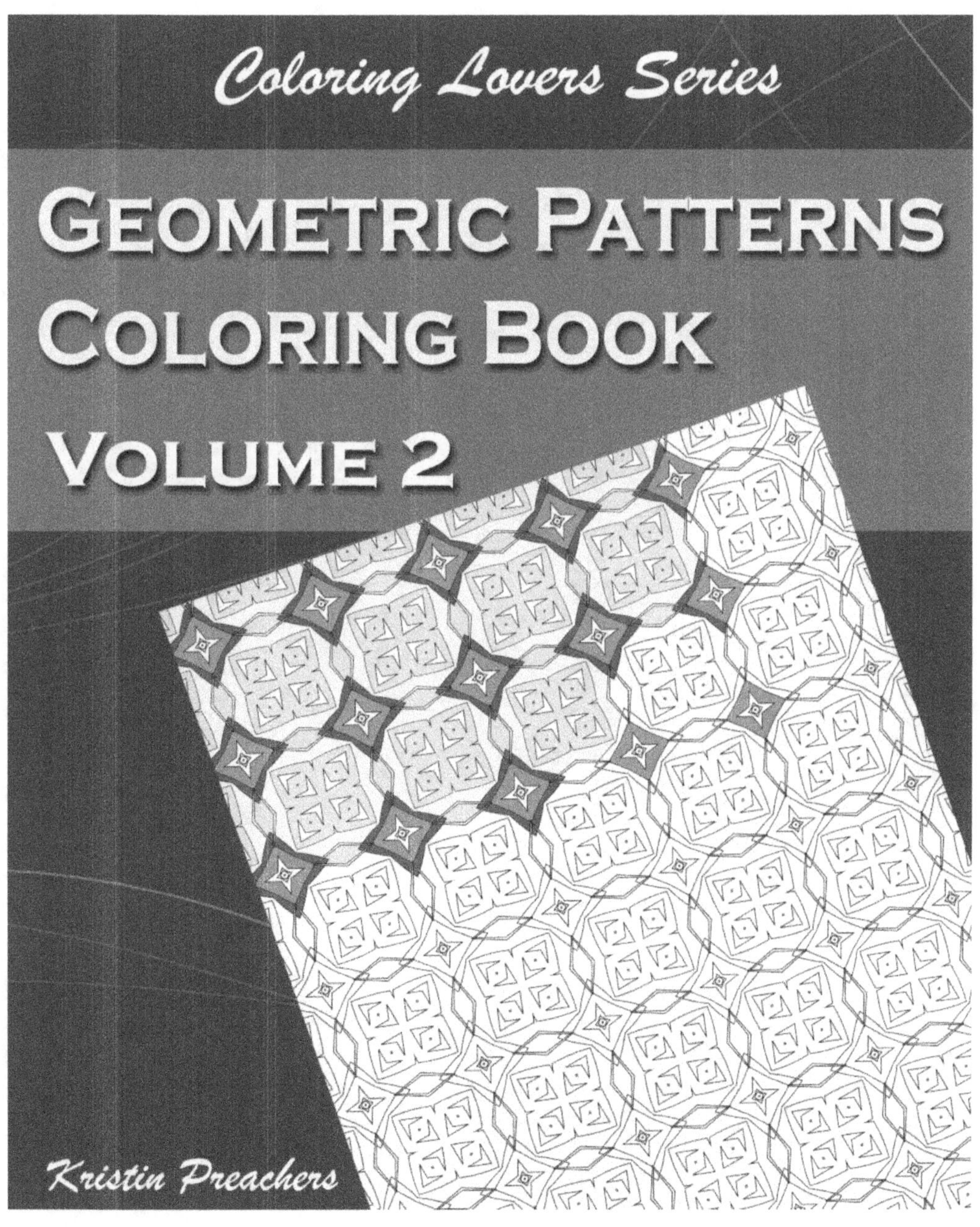